PIANO · VOCAL · GUITAR

HILLSONG UNITED

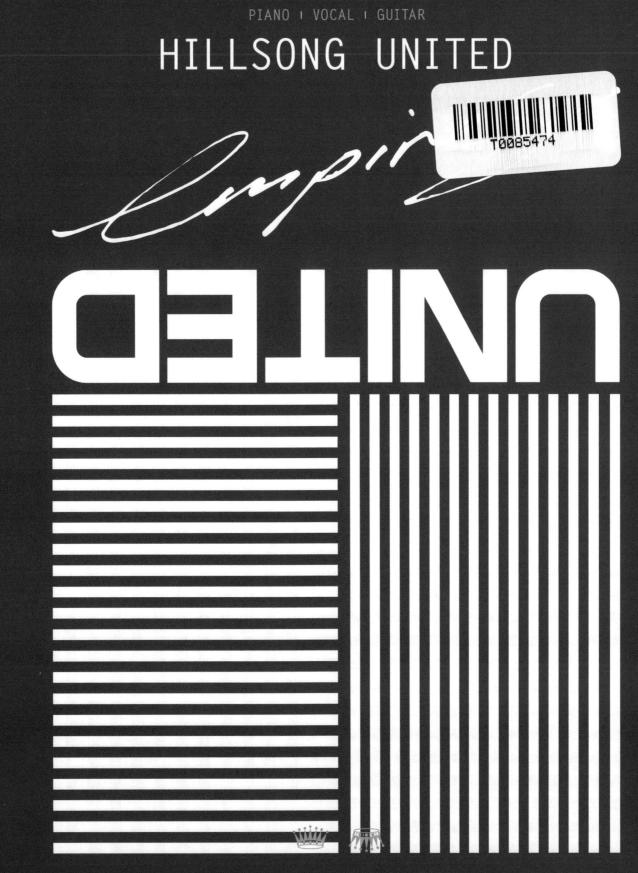

ISBN 978-1-4950-5939-1

HAL·LEONARD®
CORPORATION

7777 W. BLUEMOUND RD. P.O. BOX 13819 MILWAUKEE, WI 53213

In Australia Contact:
Hal Leonard Australia Pty. Ltd.
4 Lentara Court
Cheltenham, Victoria, 3192 Australia
Email: ausadmin@halleonard.com.au

Visit Hal Leonard Online at
www.halleonard.com

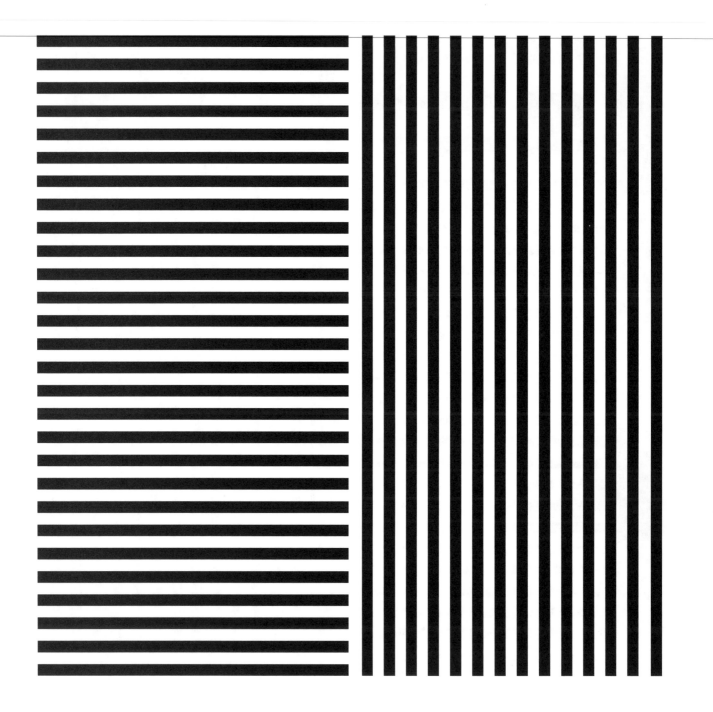

CONTENTS

HERE NOW
(Madness)

Words and Music by JOEL HOUSTON
and MICHAEL GUY CHISLETT

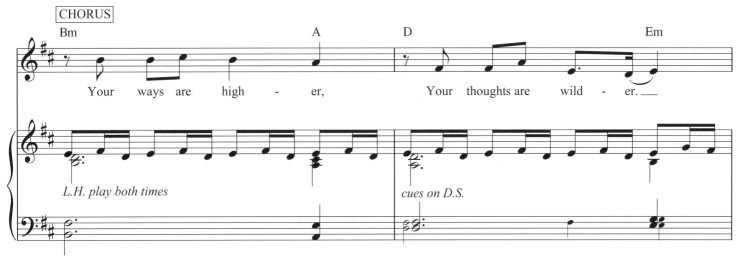

CHORUS

Bm / A / D / Em

Your ways are high-er, Your thoughts are wild-er.

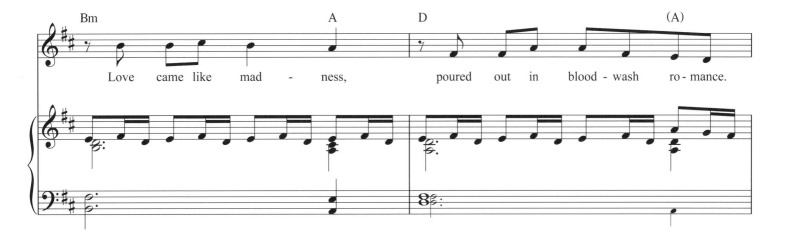

Bm / A / D / (A)

Love came like mad-ness, poured out in blood-wash ro-mance.

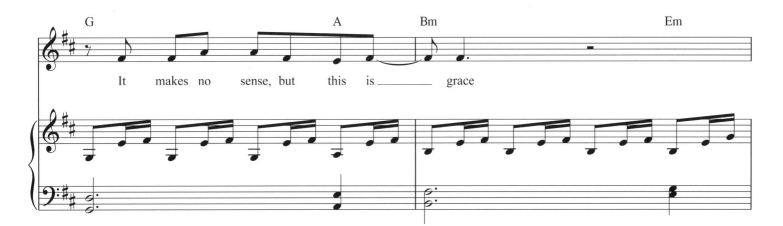

G / A / Bm / Em

It makes no sense, but this is _____ grace

To Coda ⊕

D / Asus

and I know You're with me in this _____ place. ___

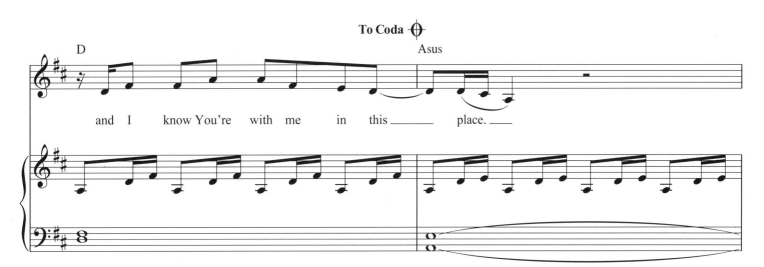

L.H. play both times

cues on D.S.

BRIDGE 1

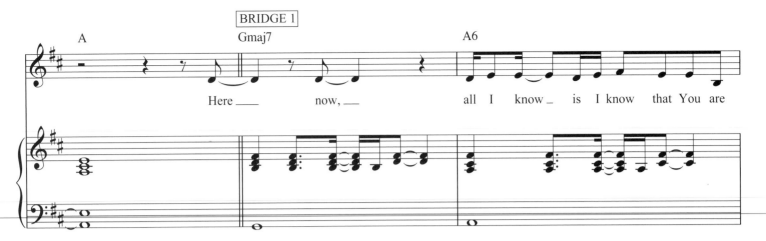

Here ___ now, ___ all I know ___ is I know that You are

here now. ___ Still my heart, ___ let Your voice be all I hear now. ___

Spi-rit breathe ___ like the wind, come have Your way. 'Cause I know You're in this

D.S. al Coda

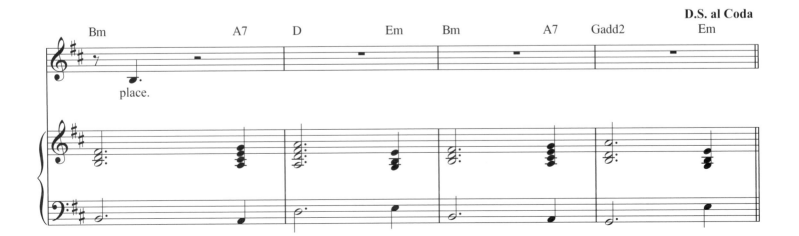

place.

CODA

BRIDGE 2

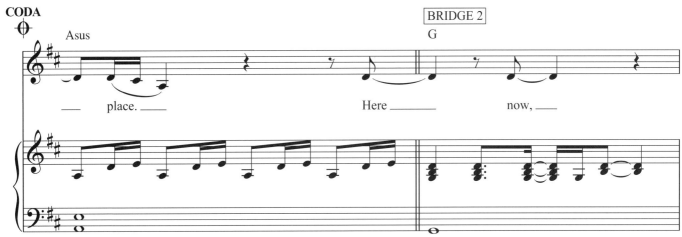

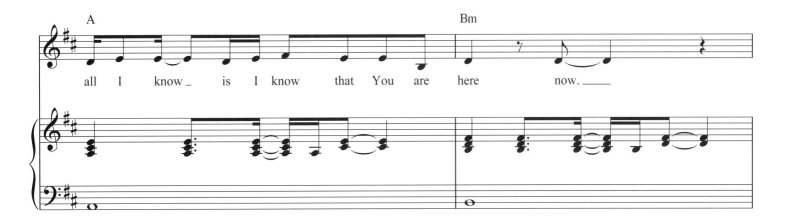

BRIDGE 3

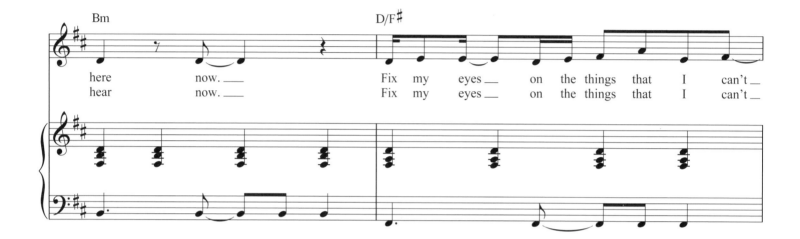

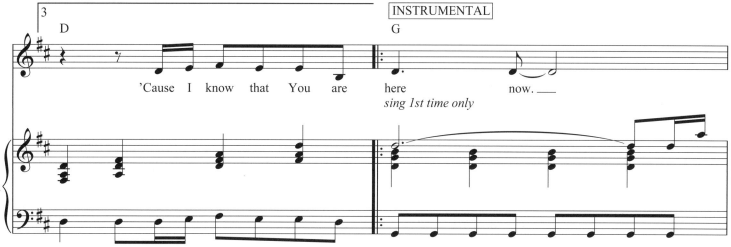

hear now. ___ Fix my eyes ___ on the things that I can't ___

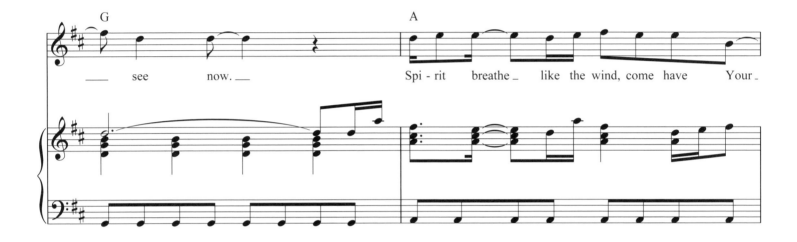

___ see now. ___ Spi - rit breathe ___ like the wind, come have Your ___

___ way. ___
(way.) _____

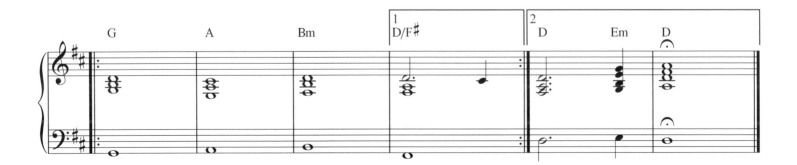

SAY THE WORD

Words and Music by
JOEL HOUSTON

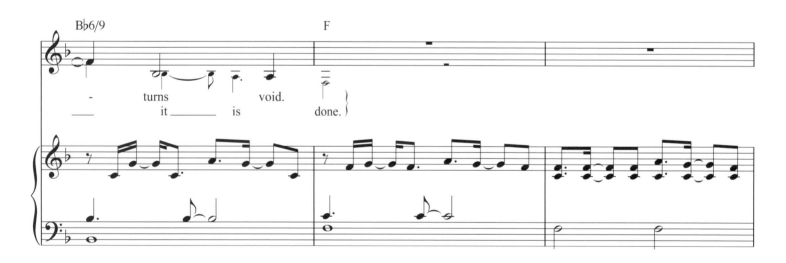

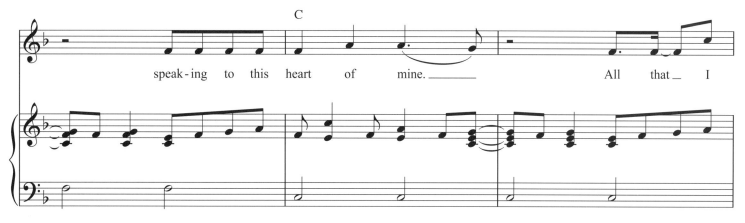

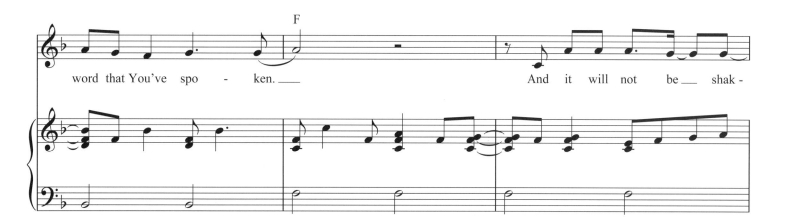

- ise, hang - ing on ___ ev - 'ry word that You say. ___

___ It will ___ re - main.

And my soul will hang on ev - 'ry word ___ You ___

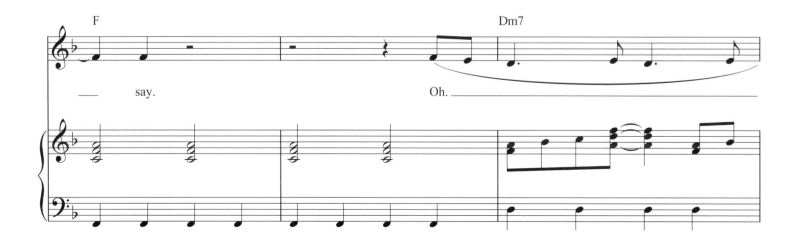

___ say. Oh. ___

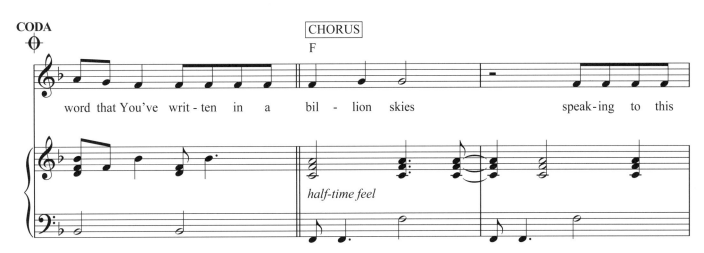

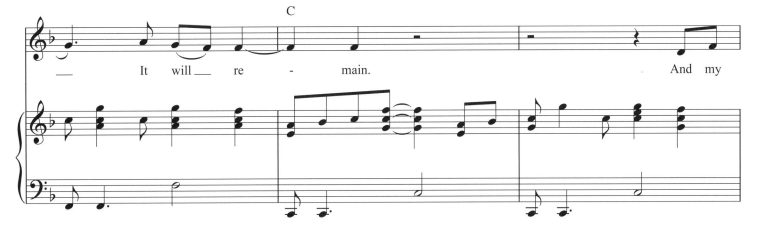

ev - 'ry word __ You _____ say.   Oh. _____

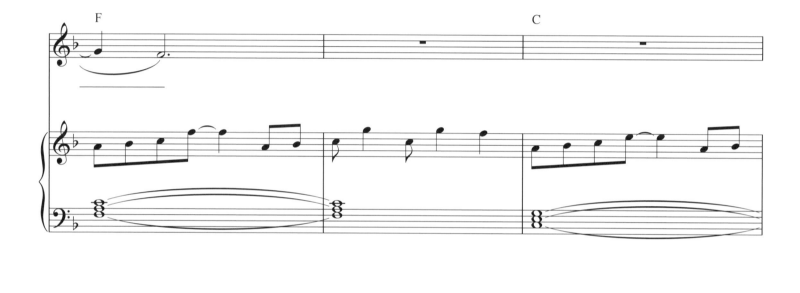

HEART LIKE HEAVEN

Words and Music by JOEL HOUSTON
and MATT CROCKER

Driving Ballad

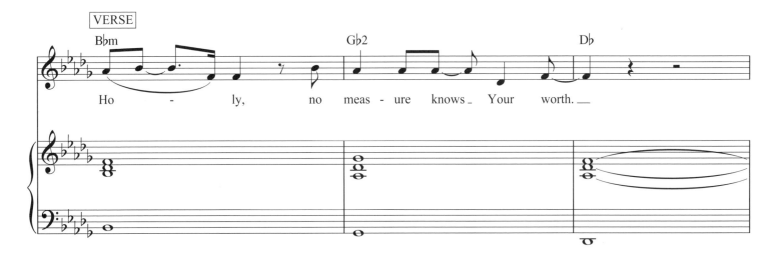

Ho - ly, no meas - ure knows Your worth.

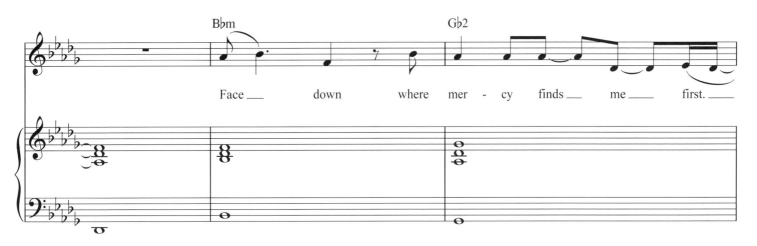

Face down where mer - cy finds me first.

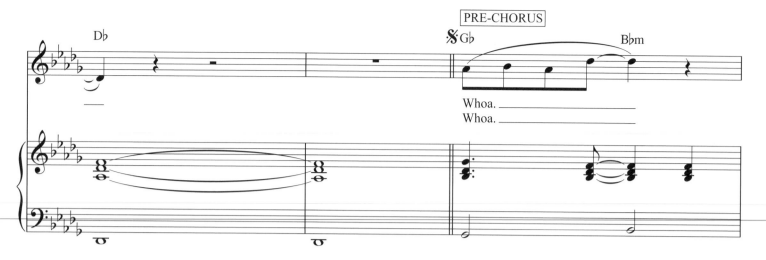

PRE-CHORUS

Whoa. _____
Whoa. _____

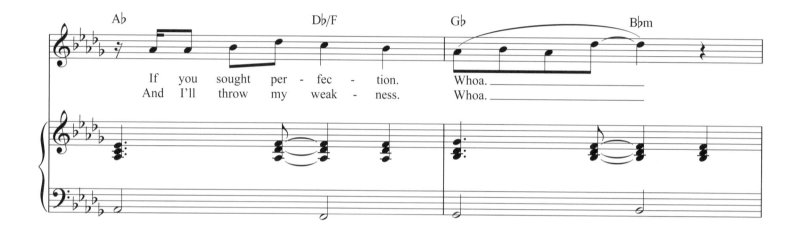

If you sought per - fec - tion. Whoa. _____
And I'll throw my weak - ness. Whoa. _____

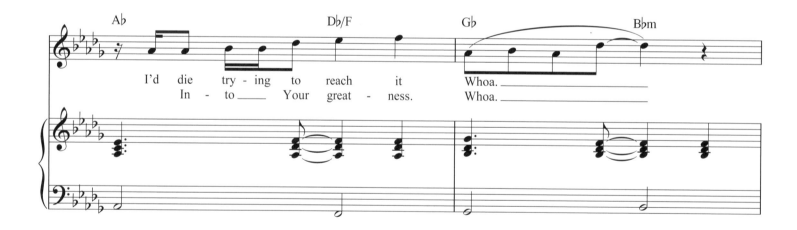

I'd die try - ing to reach it Whoa. _____
In - to _____ Your great - ness. Whoa. _____

But this bro - ken heart is all _____ You _____ want. _____
If this bro - ken heart is all _____ You _____ want. _____

CHORUS

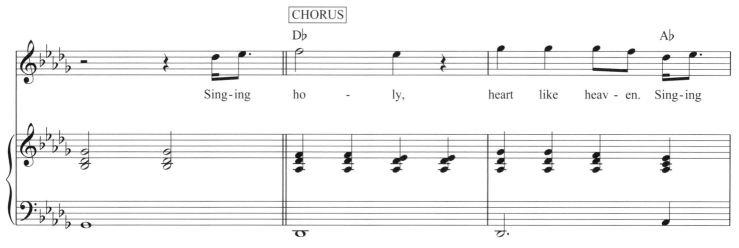

Sing-ing ho - ly, heart like heav - en. Sing-ing

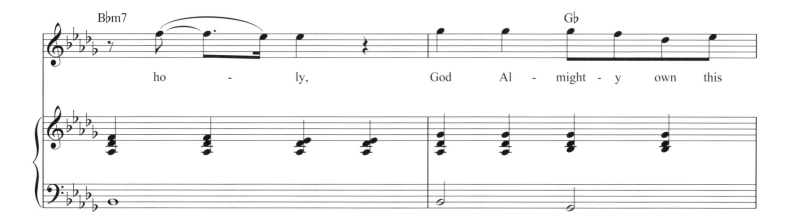

ho - ly, God Al - might - y own this

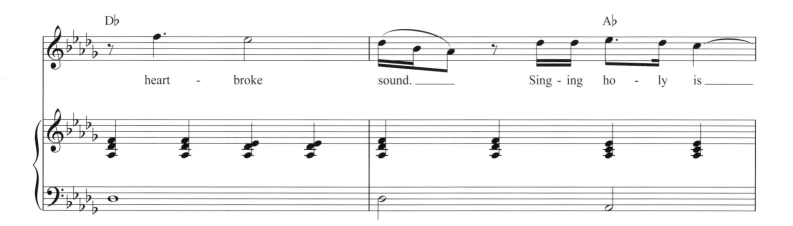

heart - broke sound. _____ Sing - ing ho - ly is _____

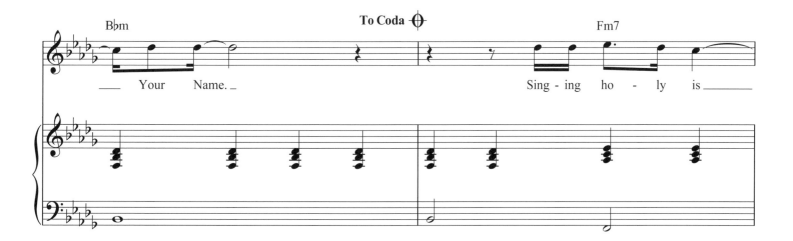

_____ Your Name. _____ Sing - ing ho - ly is _____

G♭maj7   A♭6

_____ Your   Name. _____

D♭/F   G♭maj7

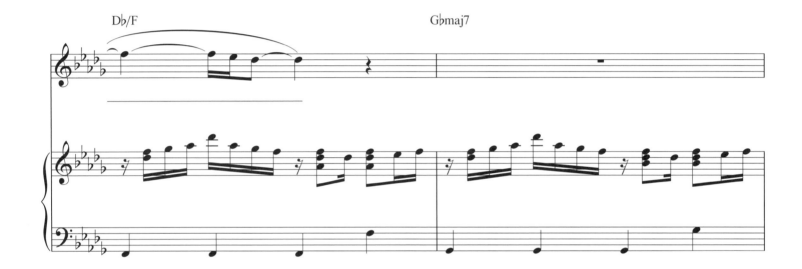

A♭6

D♭/F   G♭maj7

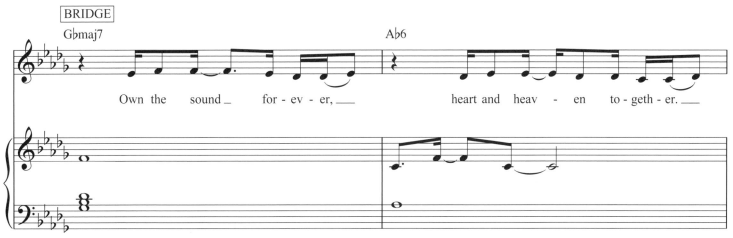

BRIDGE

Own the sound __ for - ev - er, __ heart and heav - en to - geth - er. __

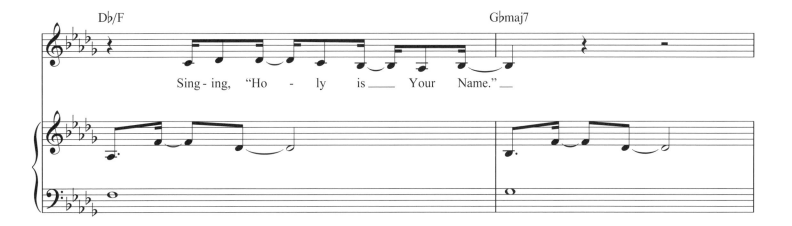

Sing - ing, "Ho - ly is __ Your Name." __

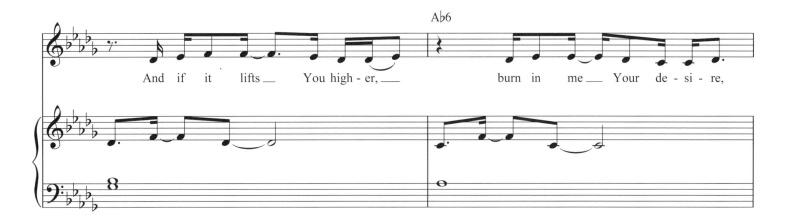

And if it lifts __ You high - er, __ burn in me __ Your de - si - re,

a pas - sion wor - thy of __ Your Name. __

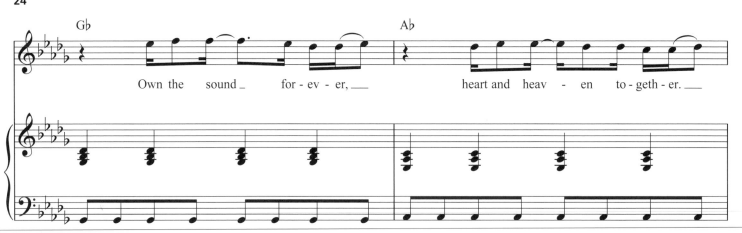

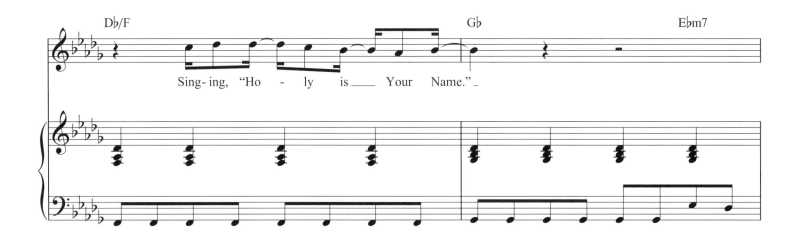

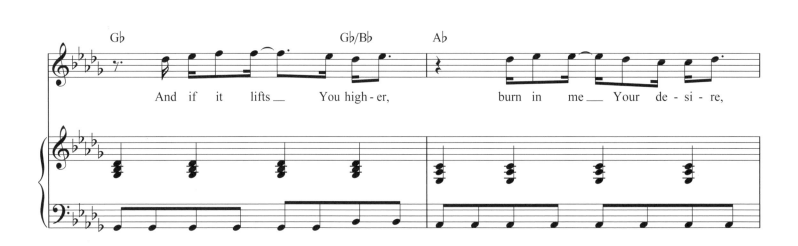

CODA

CHORUS

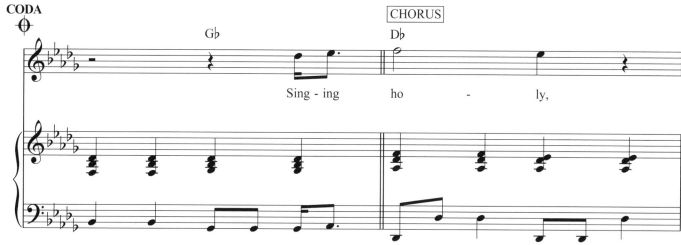

Sing - ing ho - ly,

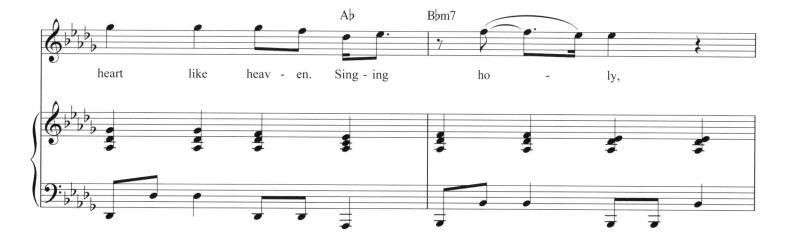

heart like heav - en. Sing - ing ho - ly,

God Al - might - y own this heart - broke sound. __ Sing - ing, "Ho - ly is __

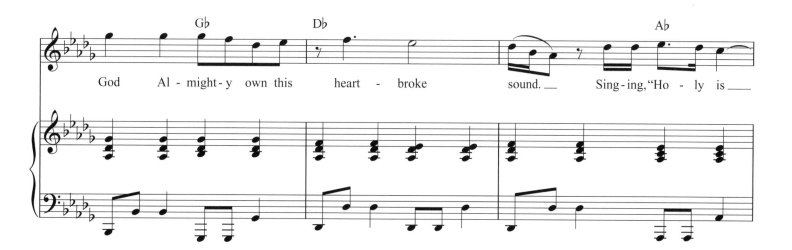

__ Your Name." _

Sing - ing, "Ho - ly is __

CHORUS

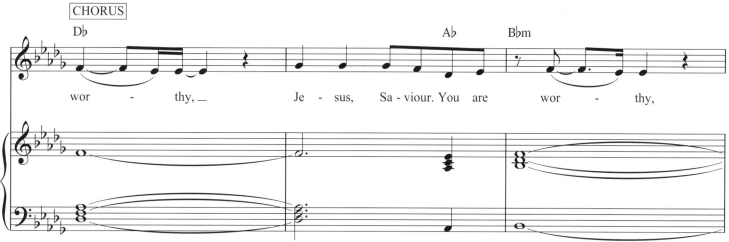

wor - thy, — Je - sus, Sa - viour. You are wor - thy,

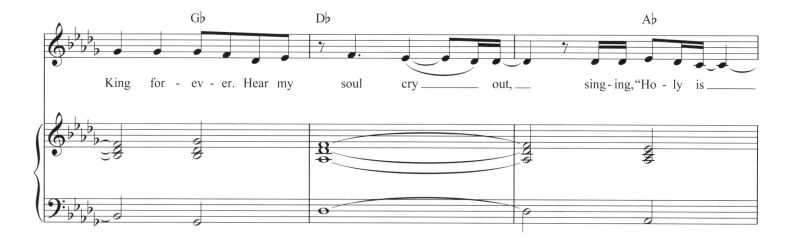

King for - ev - er. Hear my soul cry ___ out, ___ sing-ing, "Ho - ly is ___

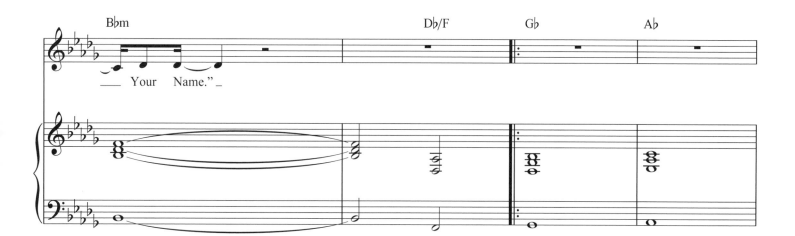

___ Your Name." _

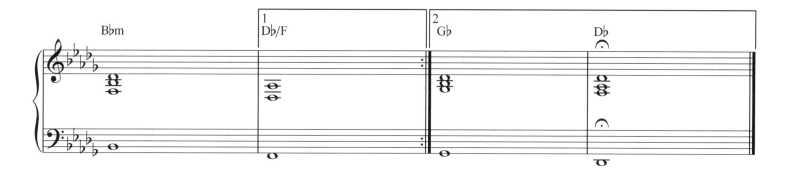

TOUCH THE SKY

Words and Music by JOEL HOUSTON,
DYLAN THOMAS and MICHAEL GUY CHISLETT

With movement

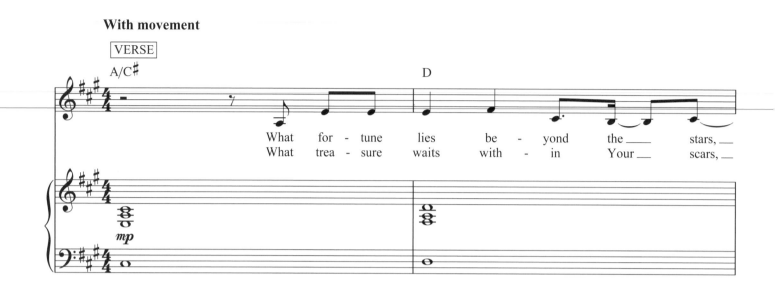

What for-tune lies be-yond the ___ stars, ___
What trea-sure waits with-in Your ___ scars, ___

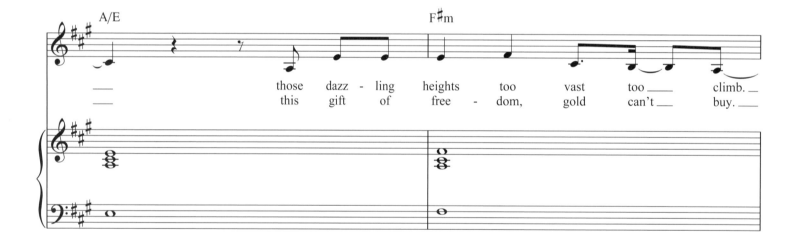

___ those dazz-ling heights too vast too ___ climb. ___
___ this gift of free-dom, vast gold can't ___ buy. ___

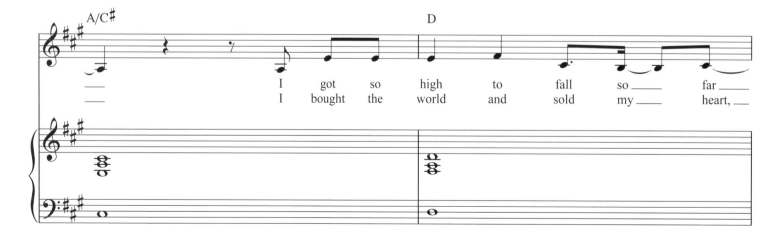

___ I got so high to fall so ___ far ___
___ I bought the world and sold my ___ heart, ___

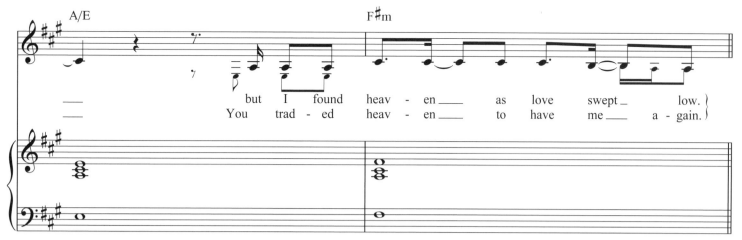

but I found heav-en ____ as love swept ____ low.
You trad-ed heav-en ____ to have me ____ a-gain.

CHORUS

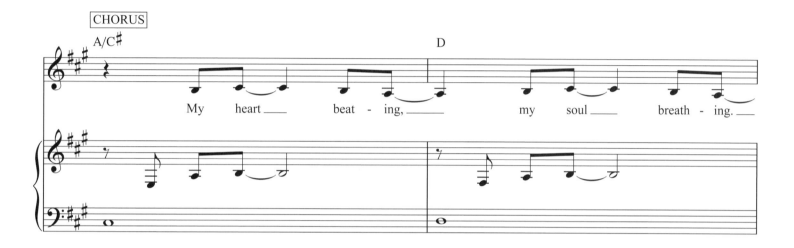

My heart ____ beat-ing, ____ my soul ____ breath-ing. ____

I found ____ my life ____ when I laid it ____ down. ____

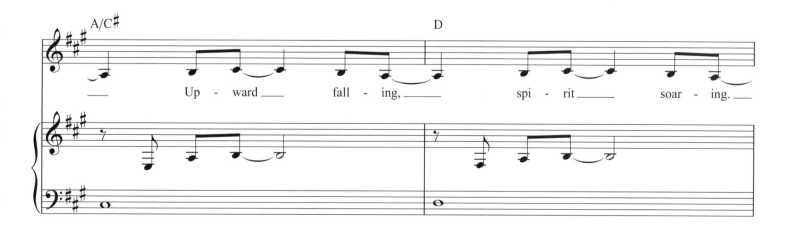

Up-ward ____ fall-ing, ____ spi-rit ____ soar-ing. ____

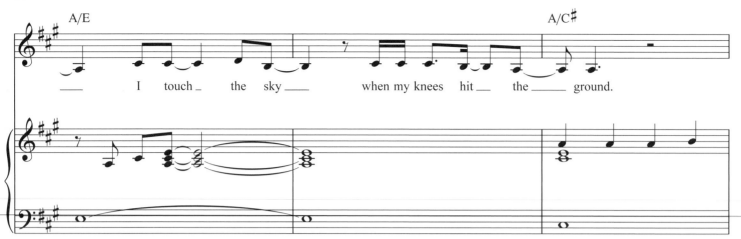

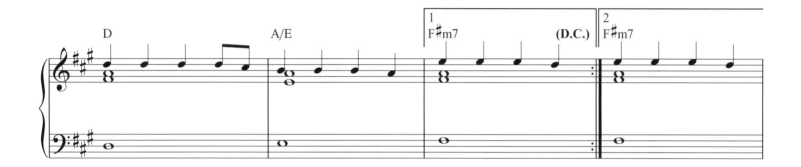

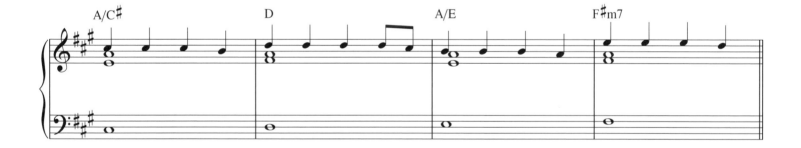

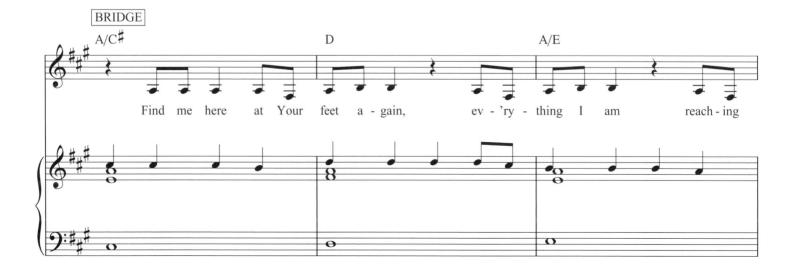

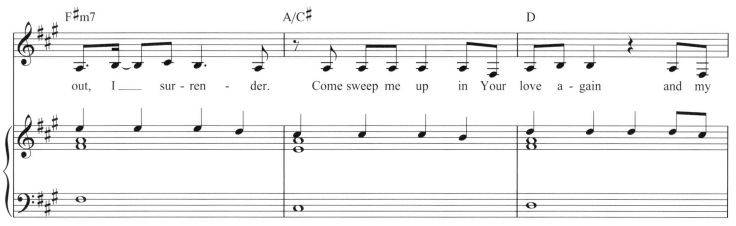

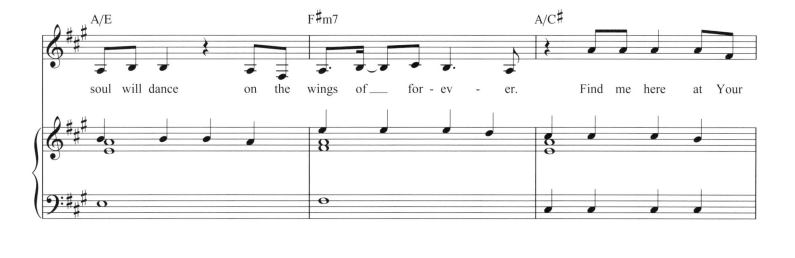

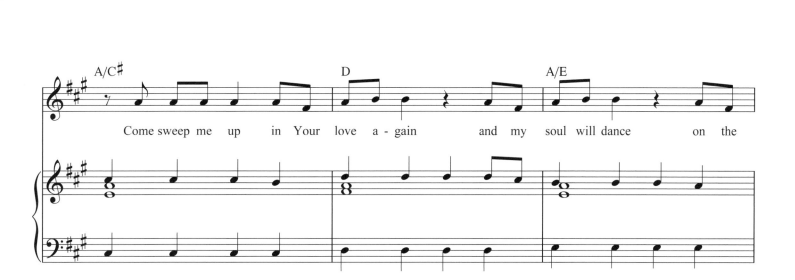

CHORUS

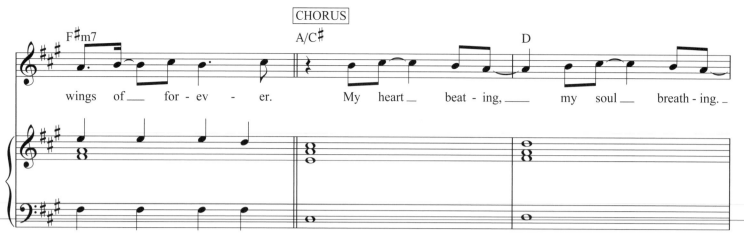

wings of __ for - ev - er. My heart __ beat - ing, __ my soul __ breath - ing. __

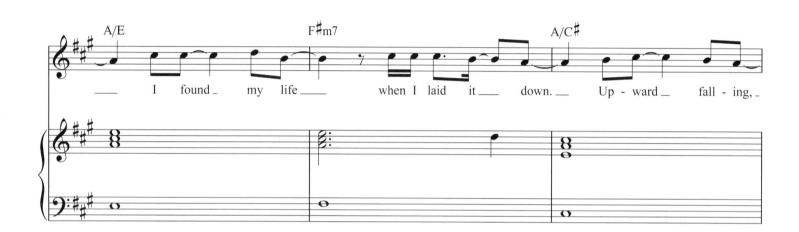

__ I found __ my life __ when I laid it __ down. __ Up - ward __ fall - ing, __

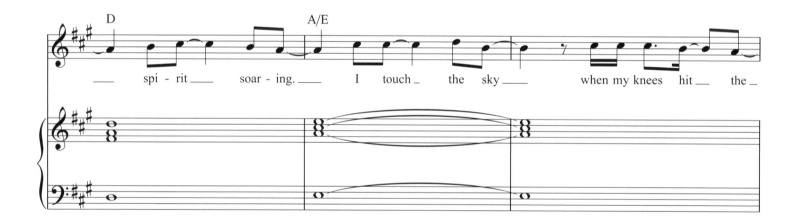

__ spi - rit __ soar - ing. __ I touch __ the sky __ when my knees hit __ the __

__ ground. My heart __ beat - ing, __ my soul __ breath - ing. __ I found __ my life __

when I laid it ___ down. ___ Up - ward ___ fall - ing, ___ spi - rit ___ soar - ing. ___

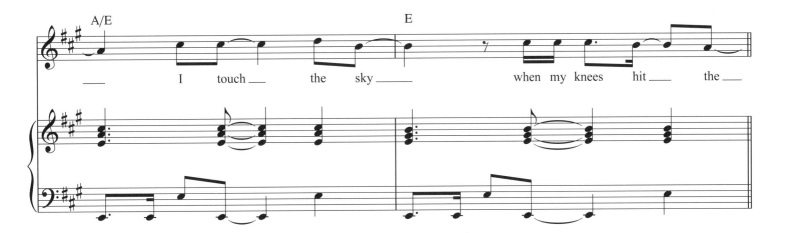

___ I touch ___ the sky ___ when my knees hit ___ the ___

BRIDGE

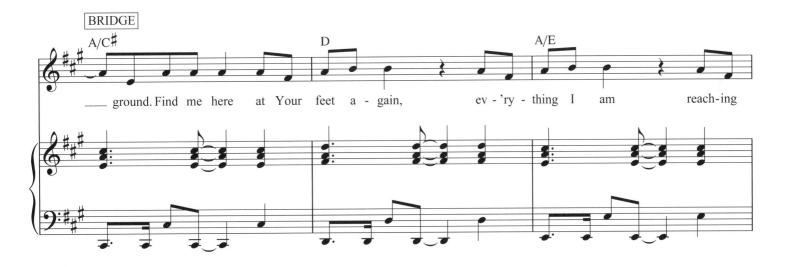

___ ground. Find me here at Your feet a - gain, ev -'ry - thing I am reach - ing

out, I ___ sur - ren - der. Come sweep me up in Your love a - gain and my

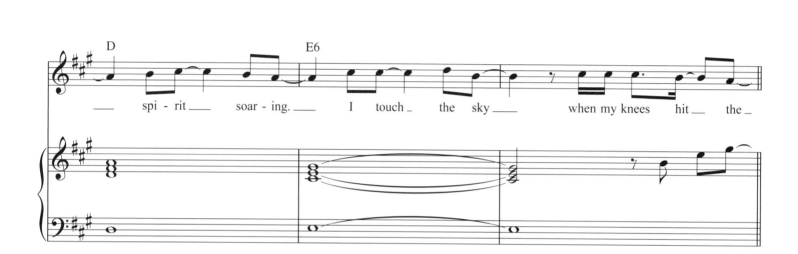

STREET CALLED MERCY

Words and Music by JOEL HOUSTON
and MATT CROCKER

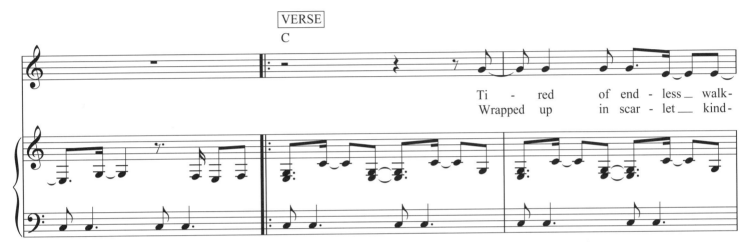

Ti - red of end - less _ walk-
Wrapped up in scar - let _ kind-

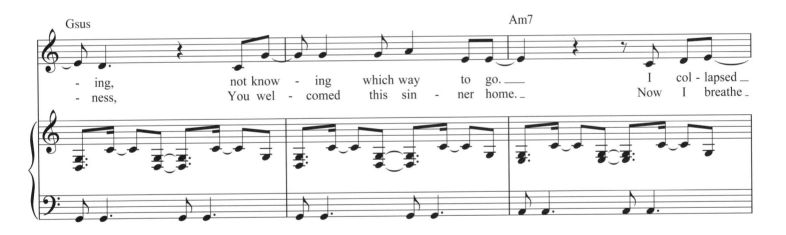

- ing, not know - ing which way to go. _ I col - lapsed _
- ness, You wel - comed this sin - ner home. _ Now I breathe _

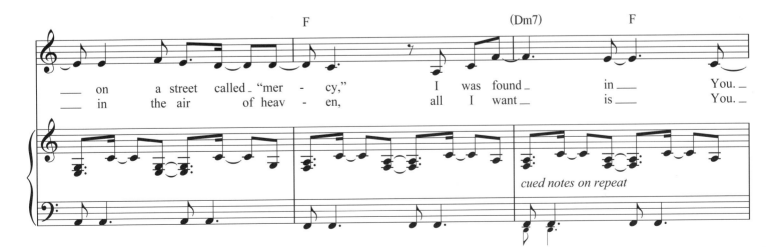

_ on a street called _ "mer - cy," I was found _ in _ You. _
_ in the air of heav - en, all I want _ is _ You. _

cued notes on repeat

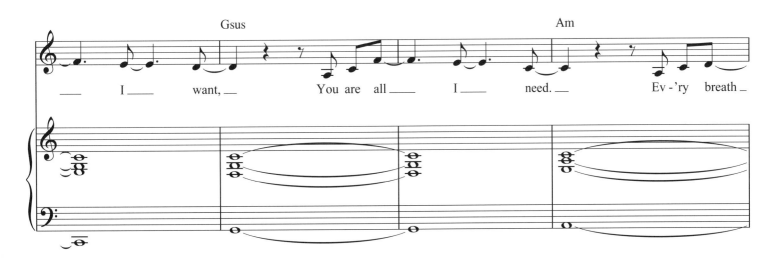

You are all ___ I ___ want, ___ You are all ___

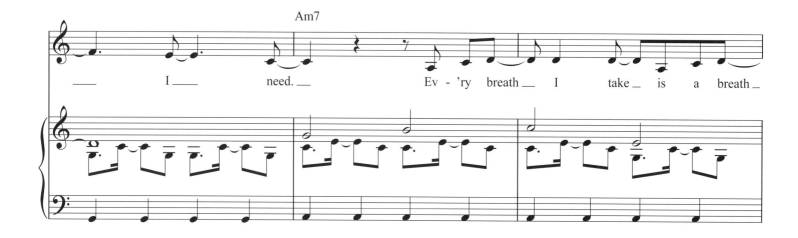

___ I ___ need. ___ Ev - 'ry breath ___ I take ___ is a breath ___

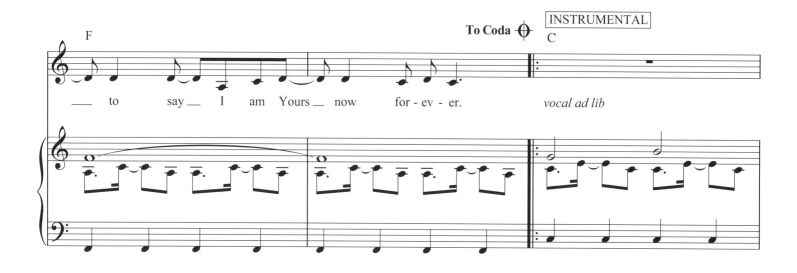

___ to say ___ I am Yours ___ now for - ev - er. *vocal ad lib*

To Coda INSTRUMENTAL

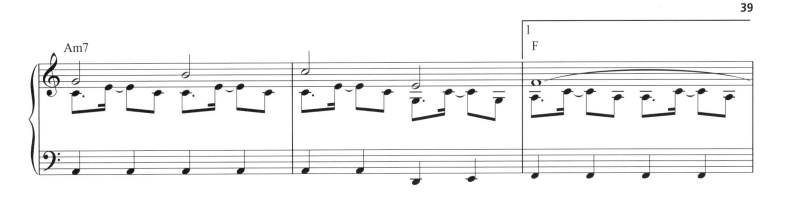

All I want ___ is ___ You. ___

D.S. al Coda

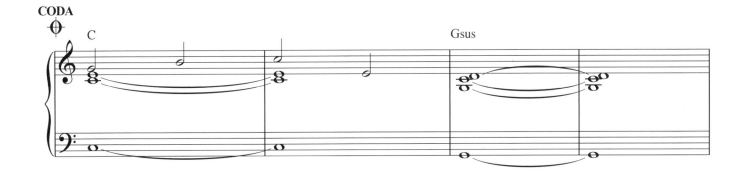

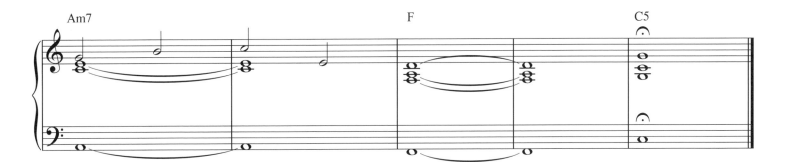

WHEN I LOST MY HEART TO YOU
(Hallelujah)

Words and Music by
JOEL HOUSTON

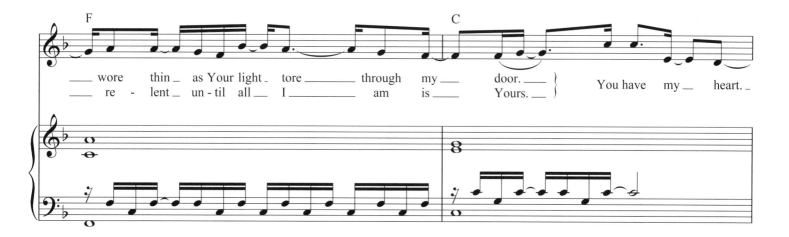

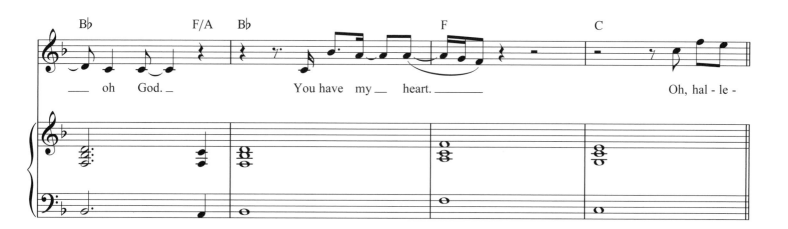

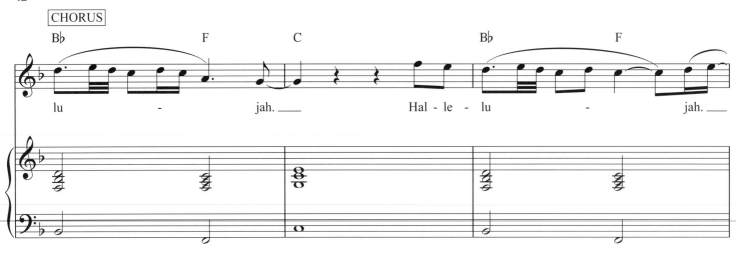

CHORUS

lu - jah. ___ Hal - le - lu - jah. ___

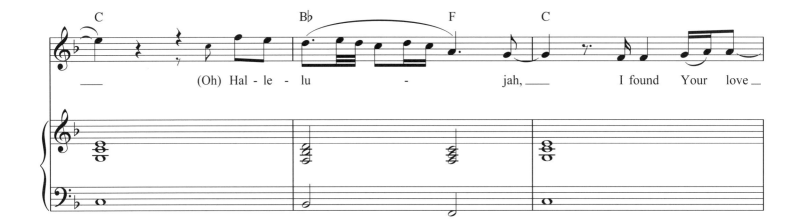

___ (Oh) Hal - le - lu - jah, ___ I found Your love ___

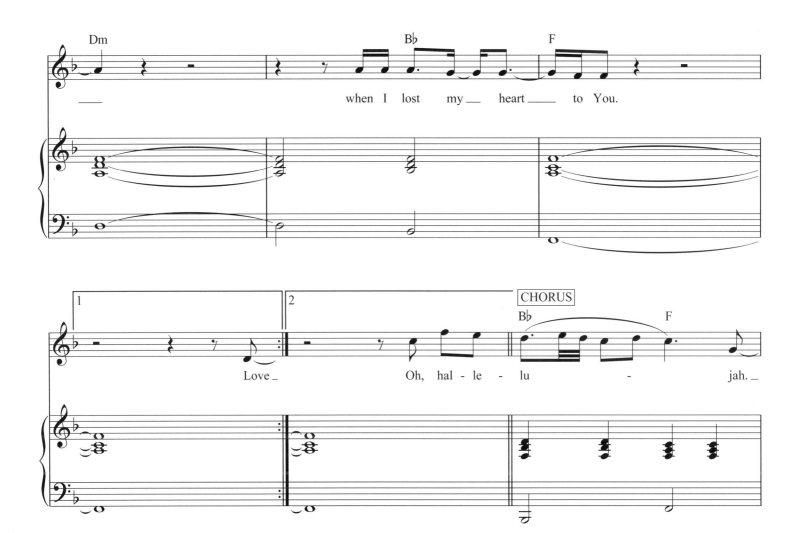

___ when I lost my ___ heart ___ to You.

1

2

CHORUS

Love ___ Oh, hal - le - lu - jah. _

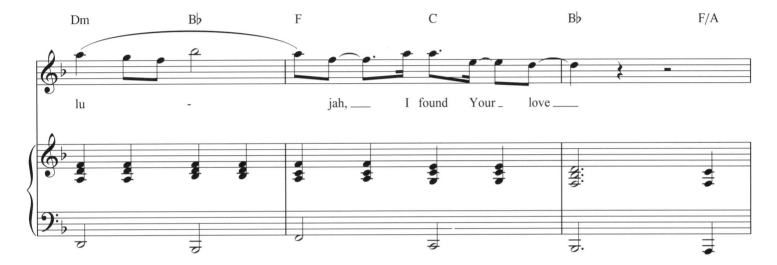

EVEN WHEN IT HURTS
(Praise Song)

Words and Music by
JOEL HOUSTON

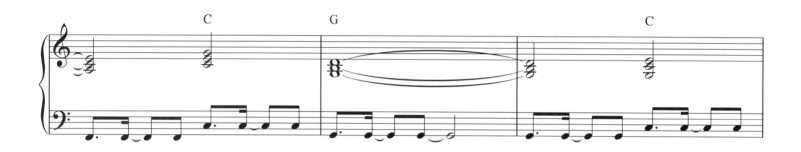

Take this faint-ed heart.
Take this moun-tain weight.

Take these
Take these

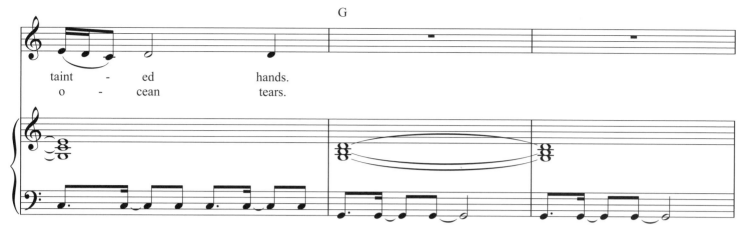

taint - ed hands.
o - cean tears.

Wash me in Your love.
Hold me through the trial.

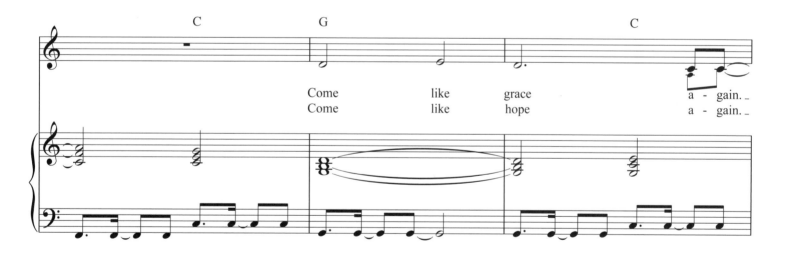

Come like grace a - gain.
Come like hope a - gain.

CHORUS

E - ven when my strength is lost,
E - ven when the fight seems lost,

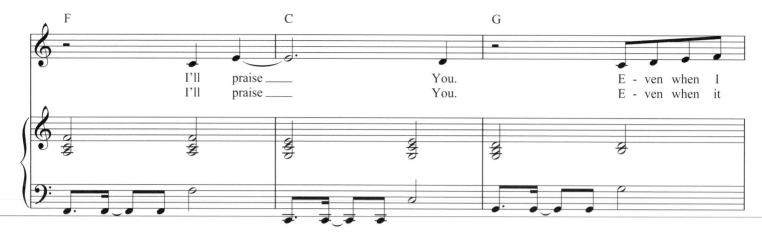

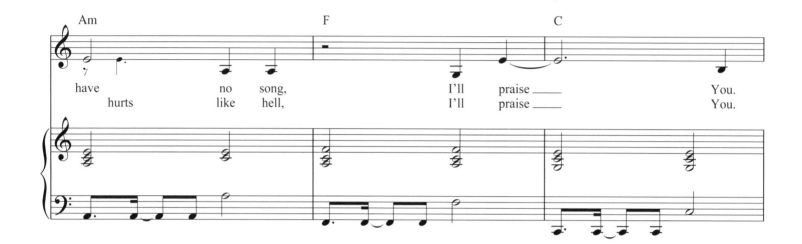

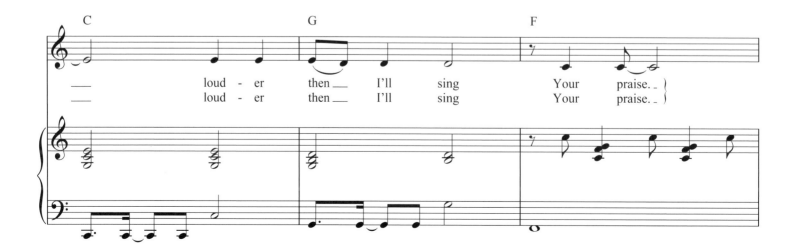

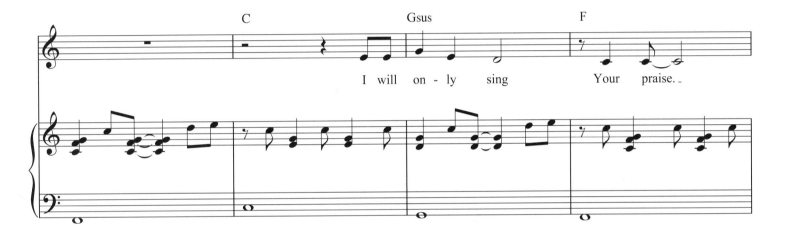

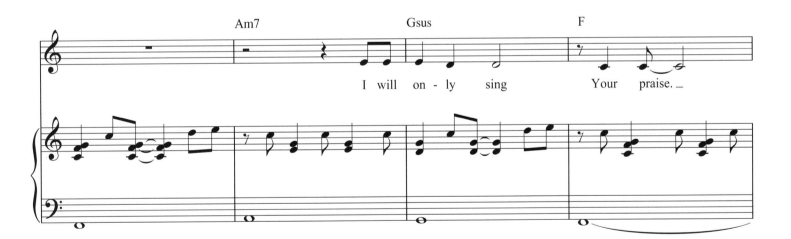

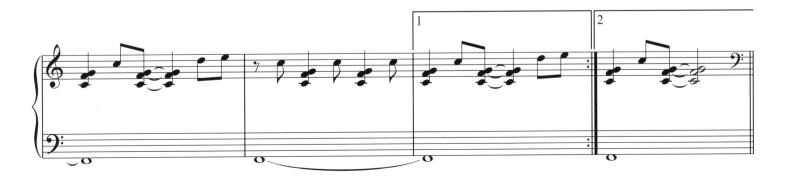

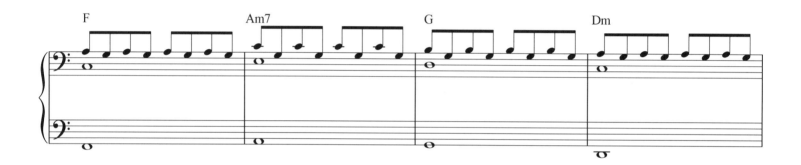

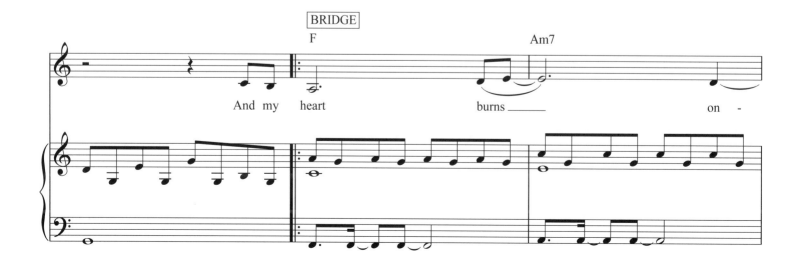

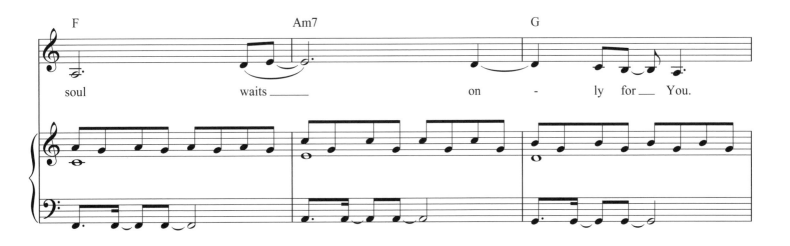

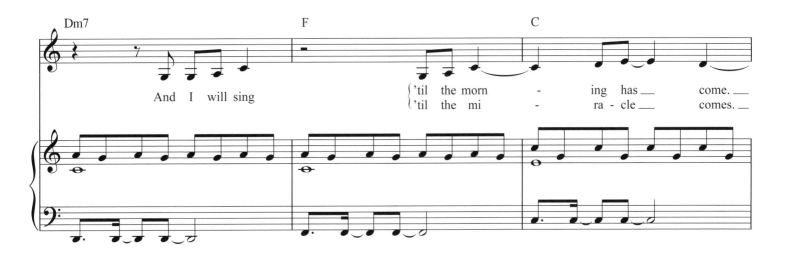

I will on-ly sing

Your praise.

CHORUS

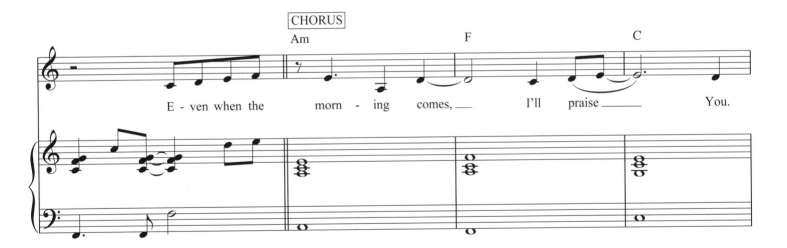

E - ven when the morn - ing comes, ___ I'll praise ___ You.

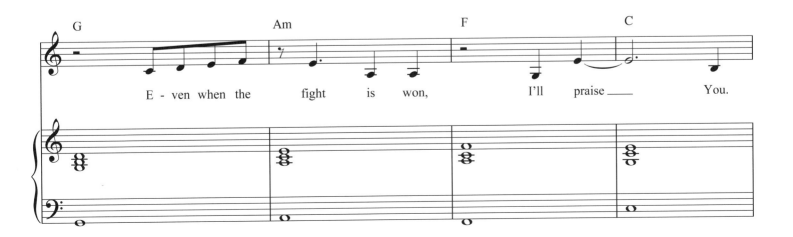

E - ven when the fight is won, I'll praise ___ You.

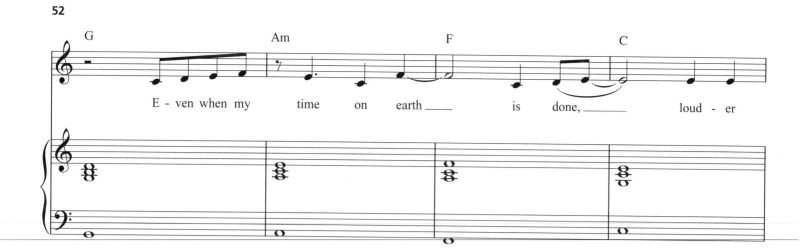

E - ven when my time on earth ___ is done, ___ loud - er

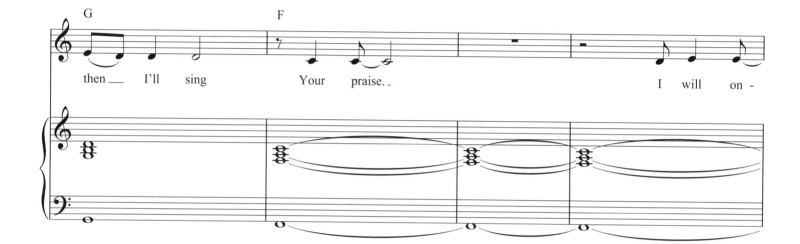

then ___ I'll sing Your praise. _ I will on -

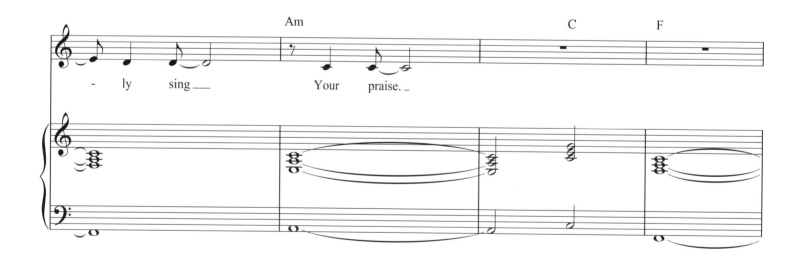

- ly sing ___ Your praise. _

PRINCE OF PEACE

Words and Music by JOEL HOUSTON,
DYLAN THOMAS and MATT CROCKER

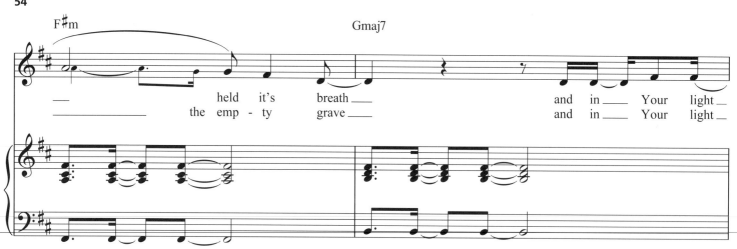

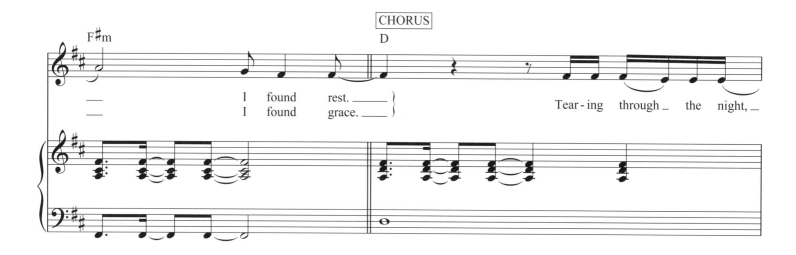

there.

And You hear   my

prayer.

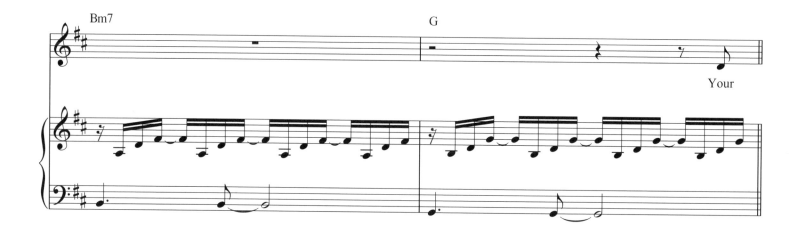

Your

BRIDGE 1

love   sur - rounds   me   when   my   thoughts   wage   war.   When
fear   comes   knock - ing,   there You'll   be   my   guard.   When When

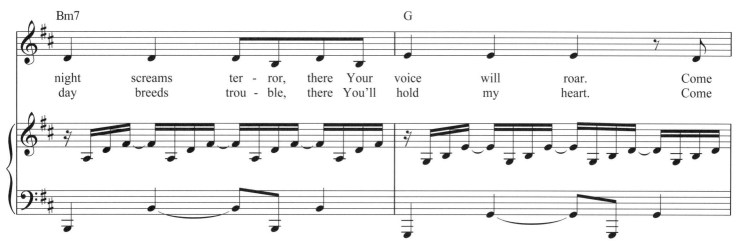

night screams ter - ror, there Your voice will roar. Come
day breeds trou - ble, there You'll hold my heart. Come

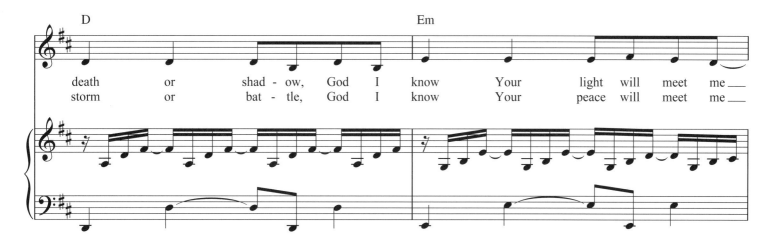

death or shad - ow, God I know Your light will meet me ___
storm or bat - tle, God I know Your peace will meet me ___

___ there. ___
___ there ___

When

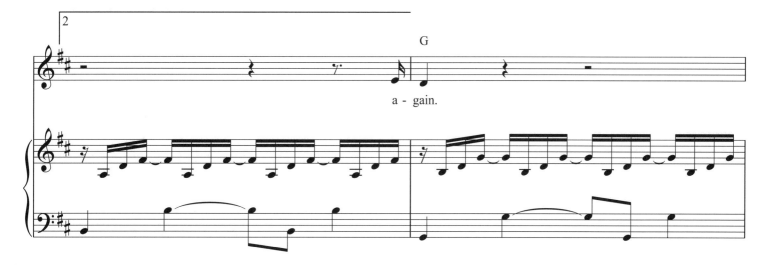

a - gain.

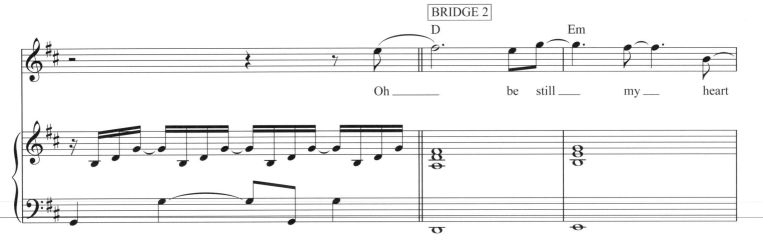

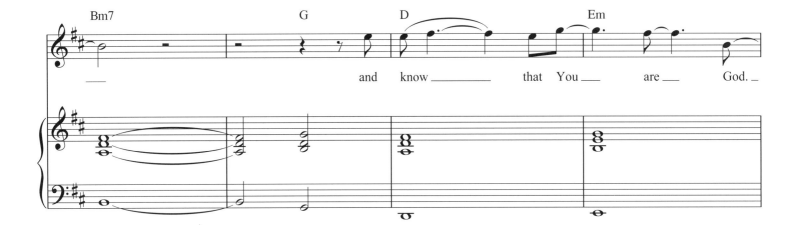

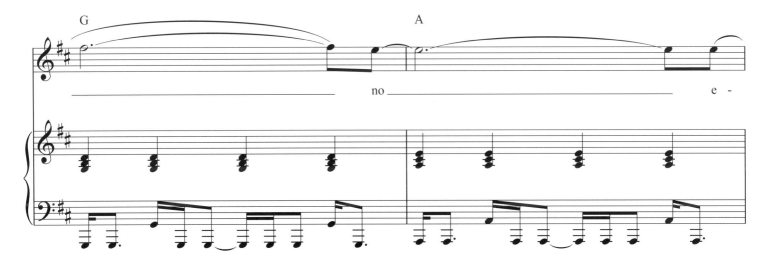

vil ___ for I know ___ You ___

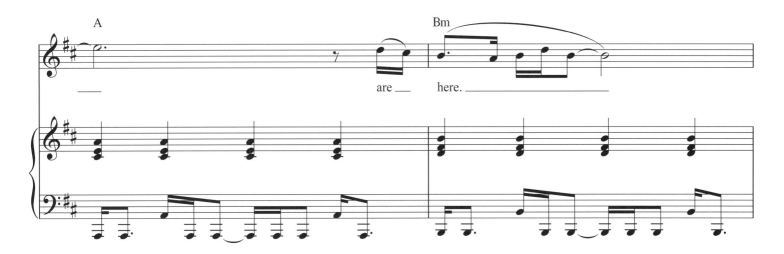

___ are ___ here. ___

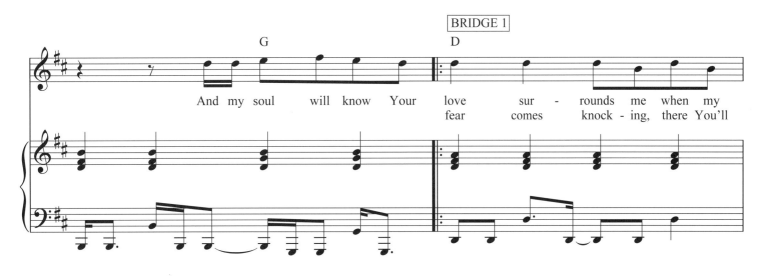

BRIDGE 1

And my soul will know Your love sur - rounds me when my
fear comes knock - ing, there You'll

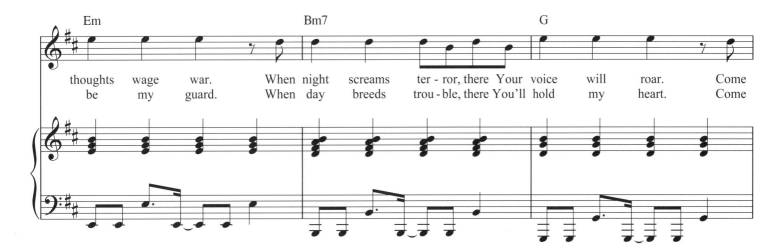

thoughts wage war. When night screams ter - ror, there Your voice will roar. Come
be my guard. When day breeds trou - ble, there You'll hold my heart. Come

death or shad-ow, God, I know Your light will meet me ___ there. ___
storm or bat-tle, God, I know Your peace will meet me ___ there. ___

And my soul will know when

Oh ___ be still ___

___ my ___ heart. ___

And my soul will ev-er know ___ that You ___

___ are ___ God. ___

And You heard my ___ prayer. ___

EMPIRES

Words and Music by JOEL HOUSTON,
DYLAN THOMAS, CHRIS DAVENPORT
and BEN TENNIKOFF

With strength

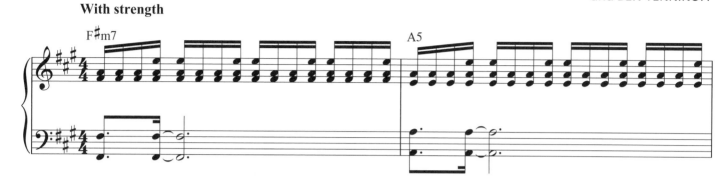

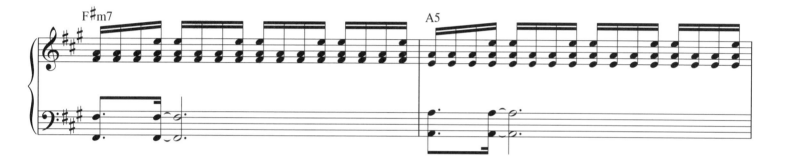

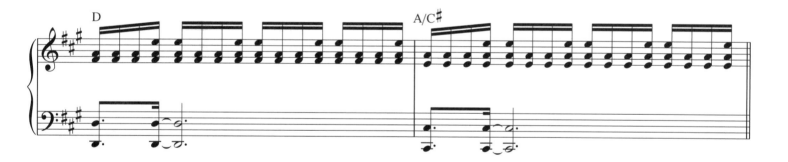

VERSE

We are worlds, we are bod - ies, ___ em - pires _ of dirt _
We are shad - ows and por - traits, ___ em - pires _ of light _

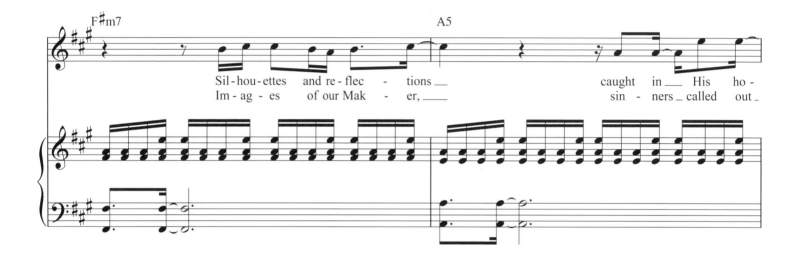

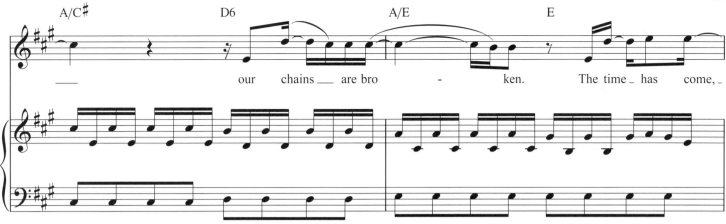

our chains ___ are bro - ken. The time ___ has come, ___

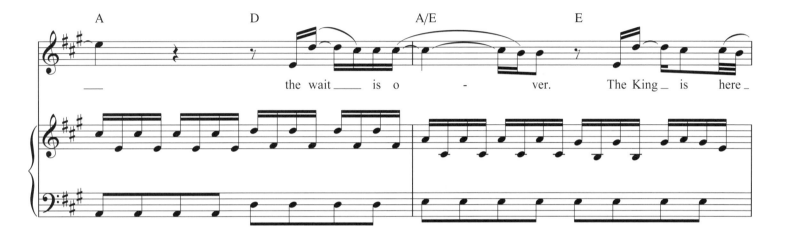

the wait ___ is o - ver. The King ___ is here ___

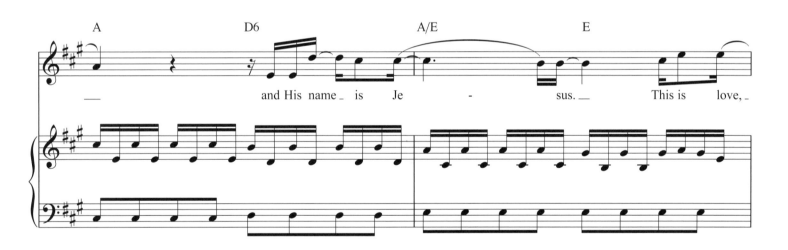

and His name ___ is Je - sus. ___ This is love, ___

CHORUS

___ bend-ing skies to heal ___ the bro - ken. This is love, ___

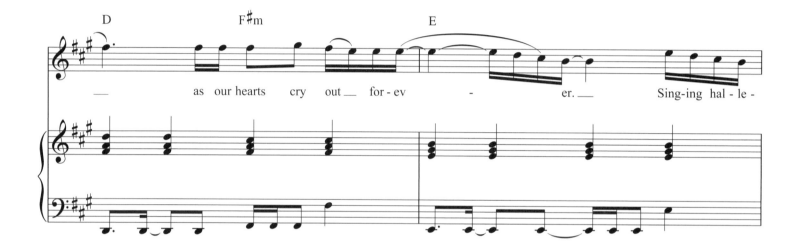

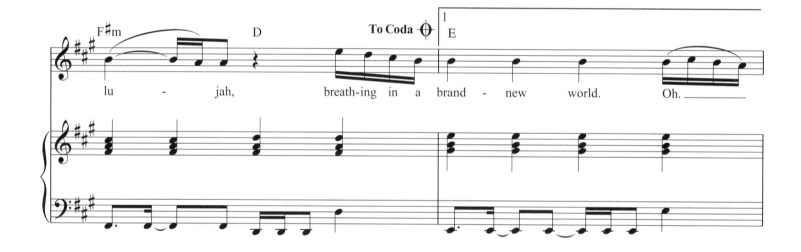

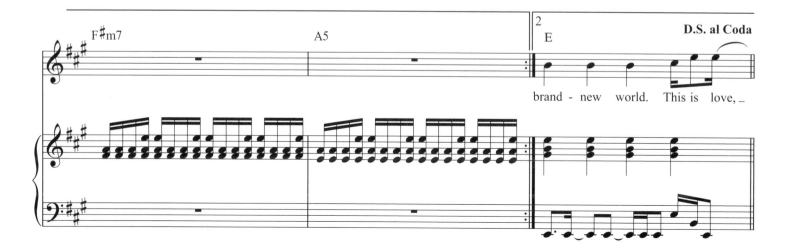

CODA

brand - new world. Oh. _____

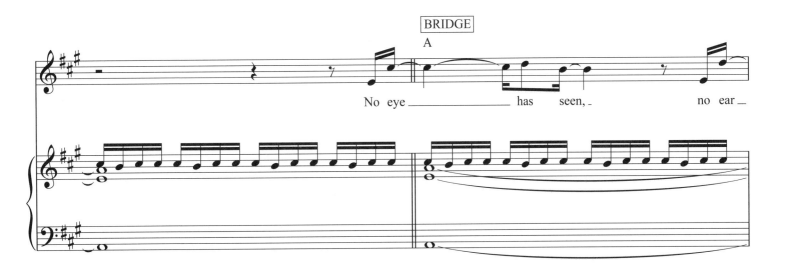

BRIDGE

No eye _____ has seen, _ no ear _

_____ has heard, _ no mind _____ con - ceived _ what heav-

Album recording continues with long instrumental section based on an A chord, finishing with BRIDGE.

RULE

Words and Music by JOEL HOUSTON,
MATT CROCKER and BEN TENNIKOFF

all ___ fear. Let Your Name ___ rule the at-

-mos - phere. Oh. _____

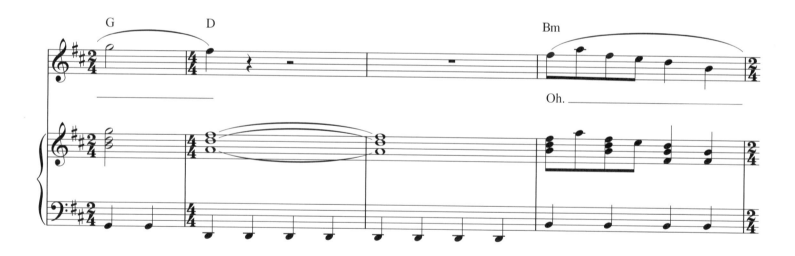

Oh. _____

VERSE

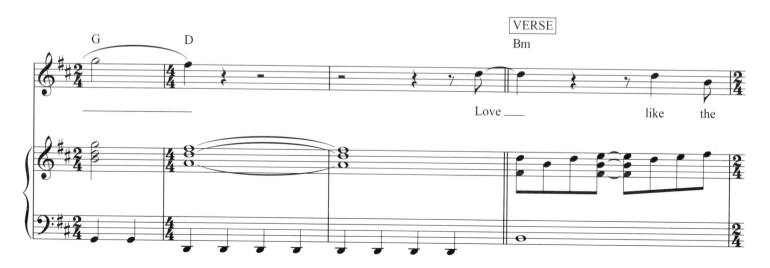

Love ___ like the

of ___ grace. Be the crown __

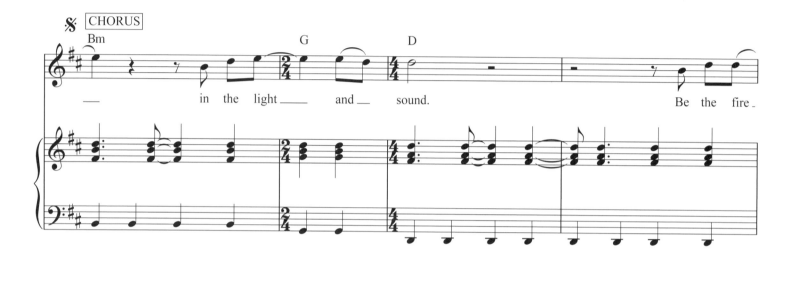

CHORUS

in the light ____ and __ sound. Be the fire __

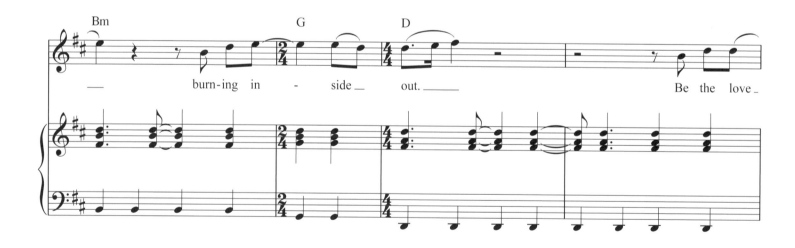

burn-ing in - side __ out. _____ Be the love __

cast-ing out ____ all __ fear. Let Your Name __

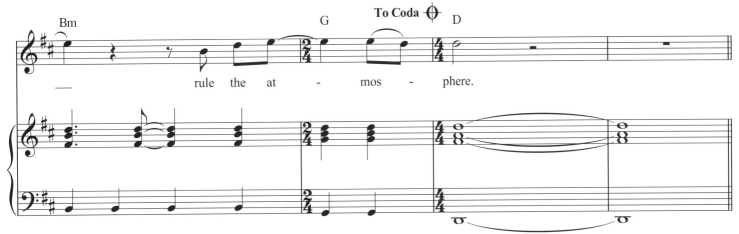

rule the at - mos - phere.

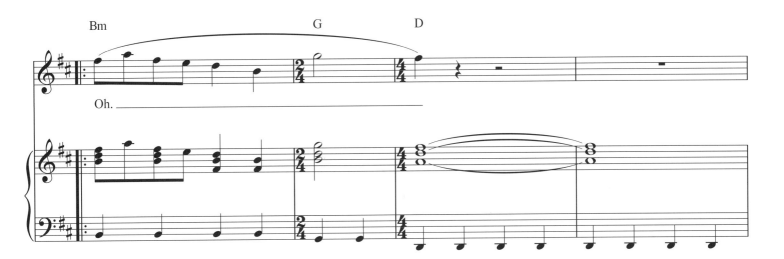

Oh. _____

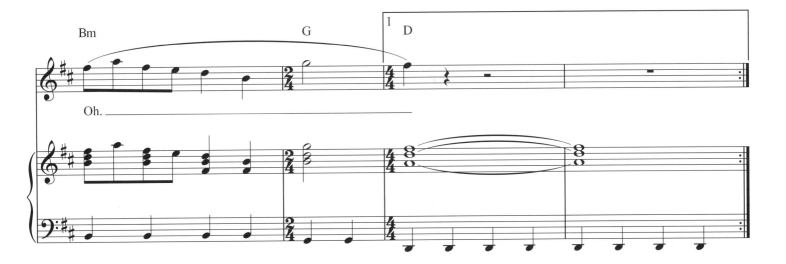

Oh. _____

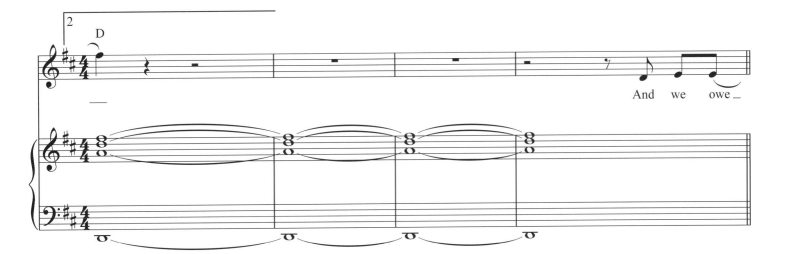

And we owe _

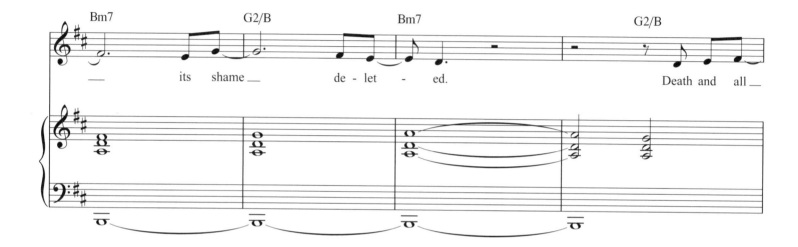

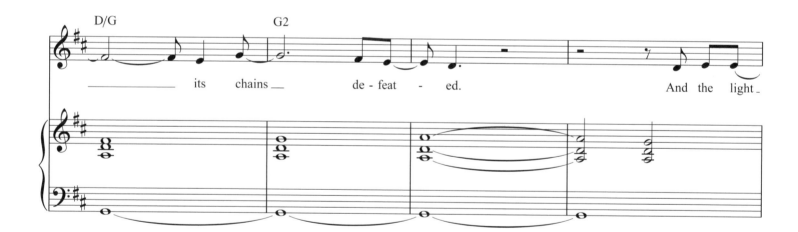

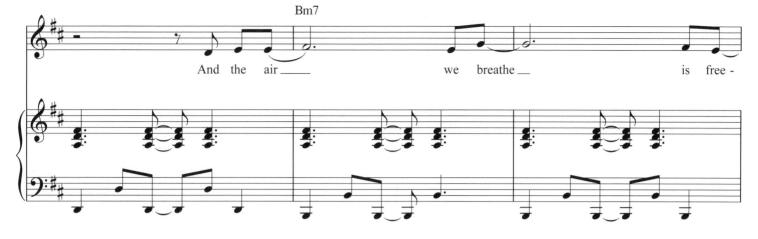

And the air ____ we breathe ____ is free -

- dom. And the sound ____ that knows ____

_____ no fear. ____ Your love rules ____ the at - mos - phere. ____

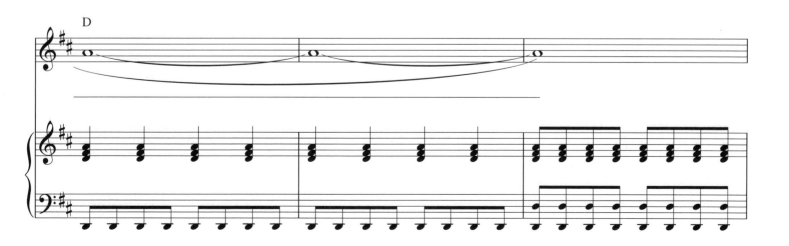

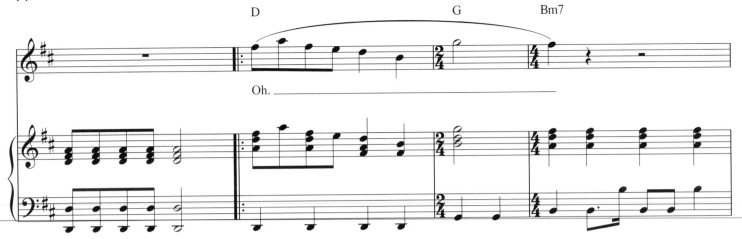

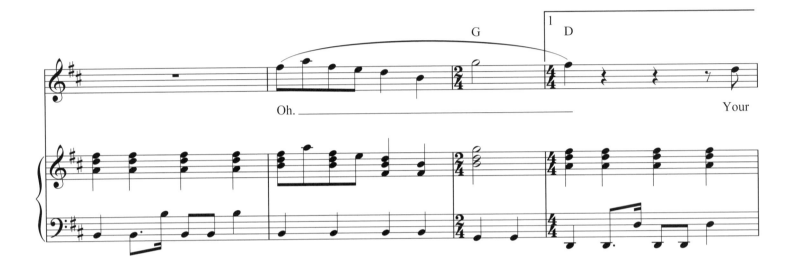

CAPTAIN

Words and Music by BENJAMIN HASTINGS
and SETH SIMMONS

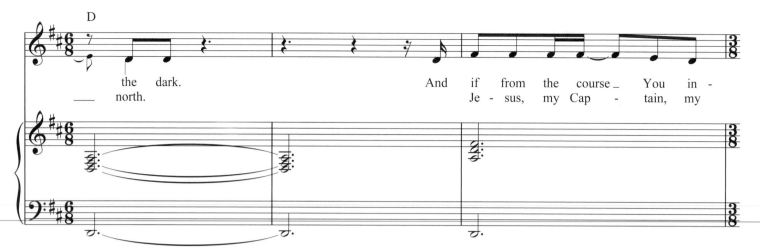

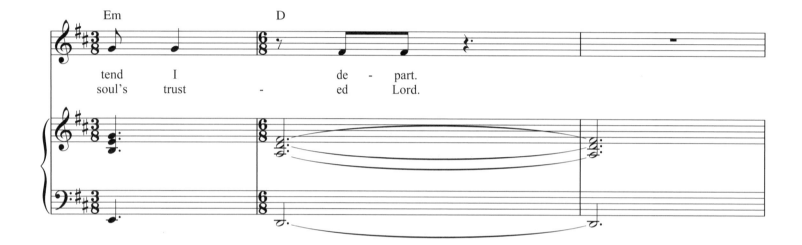

skies _____ be-fore ___ me. ___ And I'll glide this o - pen

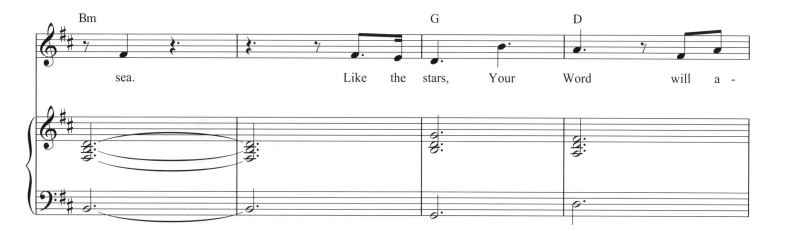

sea. Like the stars, Your Word will a -

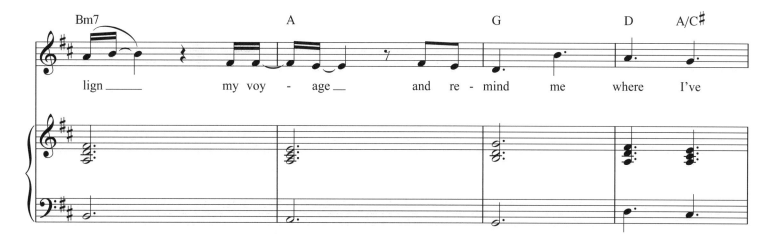

lign _____ my voy - age ___ and re - mind me where I've

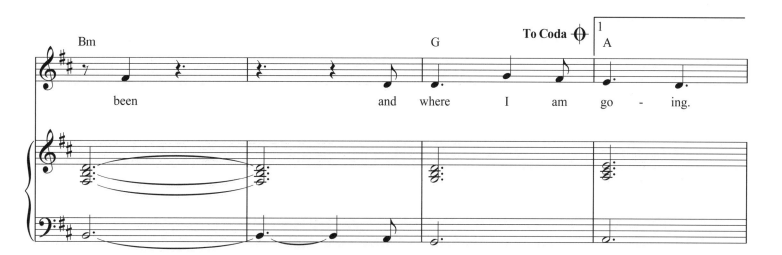

been and where I am go - ing.

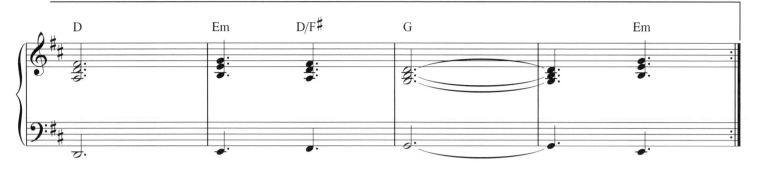

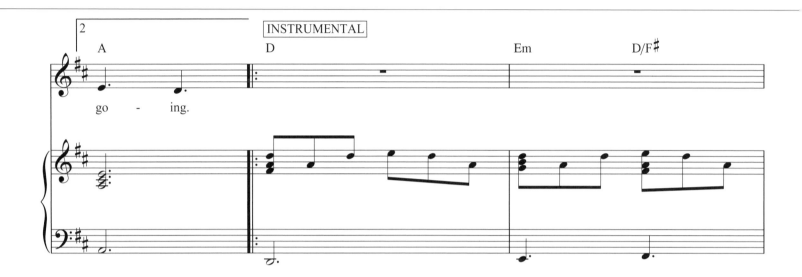

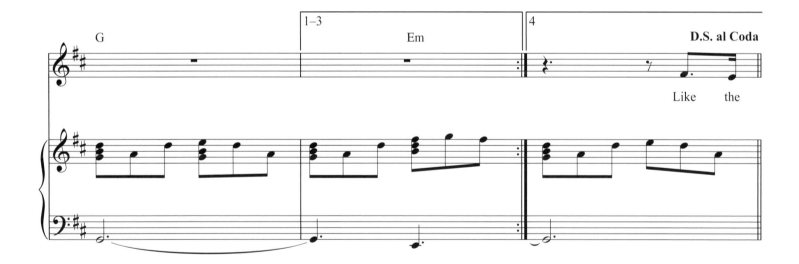

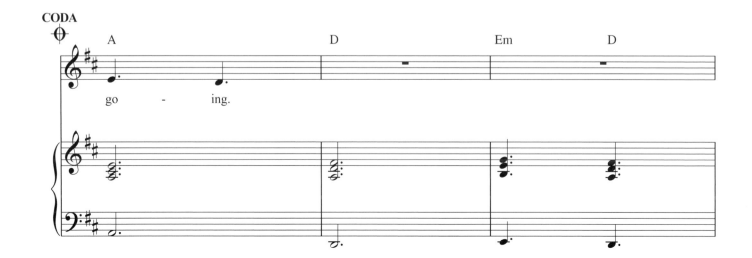

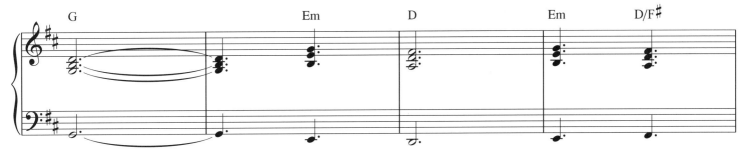

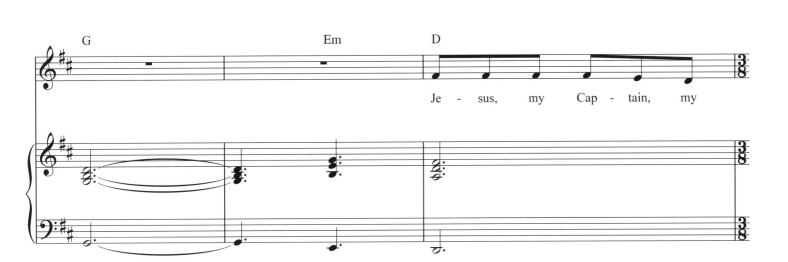

Je - sus, my Cap - tain, my

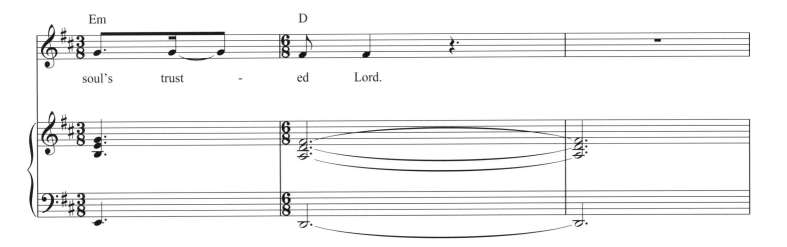

soul's trust - ed Lord.

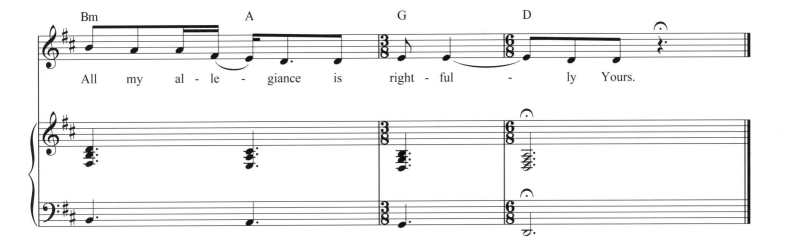

All my al - le - giance is right - ful - ly Yours.

CLOSER THAN YOU KNOW

Words and Music by JOEL HOUSTON,
MATT CROCKER and MICHAEL GUY CHISLETT

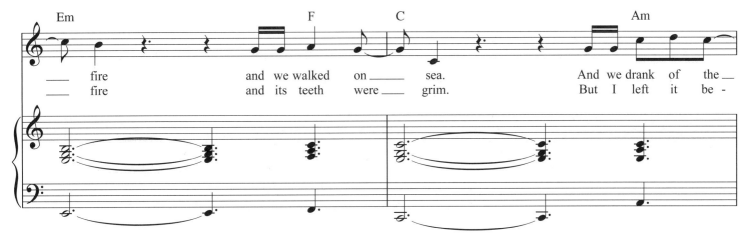

___ fire and we walked on _____ sea. And we drank of the __
___ fire and its teeth were _____ grim. But I left it be -

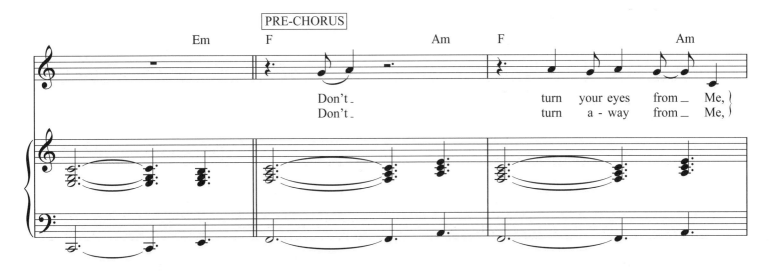

___ wine that was made of _____ Me.
- hind a - long with all your _____ sin.

PRE-CHORUS

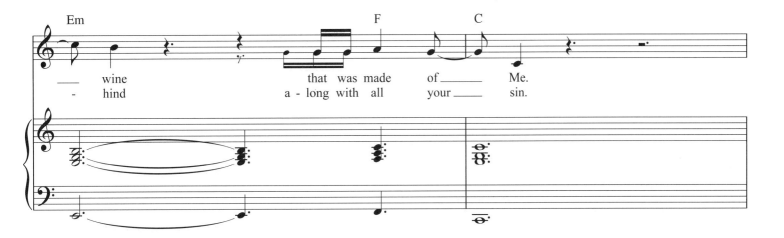

Don't __ turn your eyes from __ Me,
Don't __ turn a - way from __ Me,

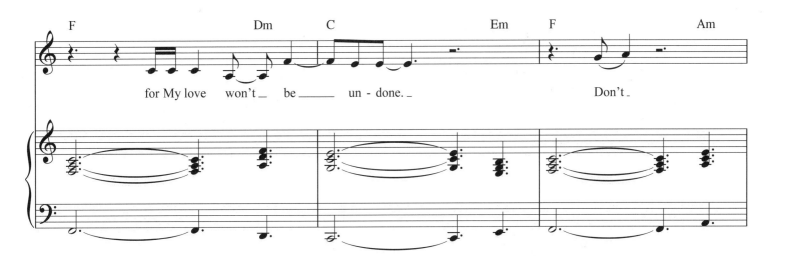

for My love won't __ be _____ un - done. Don't __

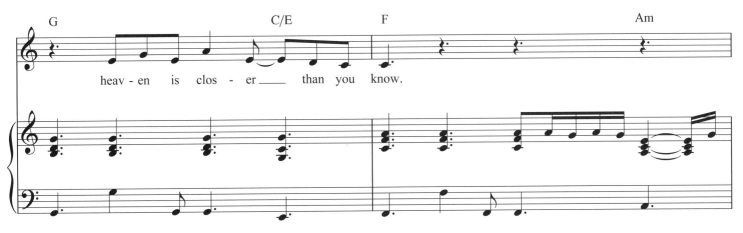

heav - en is clos - er ____ than you know.

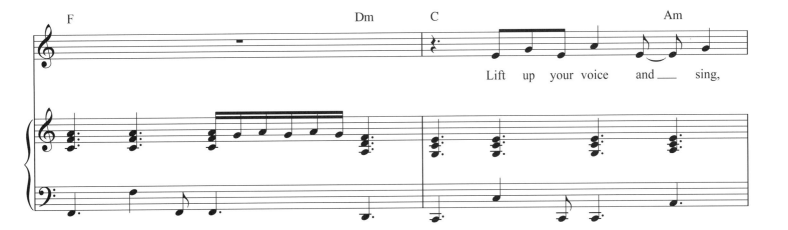

Lift up your voice and ____ sing,

know that My love won't ____ let you go

and I won't for - sake you. ____ Lift up your eyes and ____ see,

come, sure - ly come.

And I'm clos - er than you know.

And I'm clos - er than you know.

sing 1st time only

Play 3 times

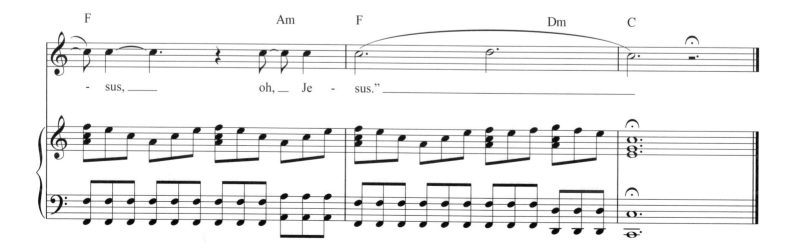